W9-AJN-325

Pebble® Plus

Let's Take a FIELD TRIP

AN AIRPORT FIELD TRIP

by Isabel Martin

Consulting editor:
Gail Saunders-Smith, PhD

Content Consultant:
Richard de Neufville, PhD
Professor of
Engineering Systems
Massachusetts Institute of
Technology

CAPSTONE PRESS
a capstone imprint

Pebble Plus is published by Capstone Press,
1710 Roe Crest Drive, North Mankato, Minnesota 56003
www.capstonepub.com

Library of Congress Cataloging-in-Publication Data
Martin, Isabel, 1977– author.
  An airport field trip / by Isabel Martin.
    pages cm. — (Pebble plus. Let's take a field trip)
Summary: "Simple text and full-color photographs take readers on a virtual field
trip to the airport"— Provided by publisher.
  Audience: Ages 4–8.
  Audience: K to grade 3.
  Includes bibliographical references and index.
  ISBN 978-1-4914-2095-9 (library binding) — ISBN 978-1-4914-2313-4 (pbk.) —
ISBN 978-1-4914-2336-3 (ebook PDF)
  1. Airports—Juvenile literature. I. Title.

TL547.M349 2015
387.7'36—dc23   2014032319

Editorial Credits
Nikki Bruno Clapper, editor; Juliette Peters, designer;
Gina Kammer, media researcher; Tori Abraham, production specialist

Photo Credits
Capstone Studio: Karon Dubke (middle left), 5; Dreamstime: Stephan Pietzko
(top), 17; Getty Images: Joshua Lott (middle right), 9; iStockphotos: EdStock (left), 7,
EdStock (right), 11, gchutka, 19, jessicaphoto, 13; Shutterstock: Bombaert Patrick, 2,
22, Eric Gevaert, 15, In Tune, 21, linerpics (background), cover, Mikhail Starodubov,
cover, Milkovasa, cover, Nadezhda1906, 3, Photobank gallery, cover, Policas, cover,
1, Rob Wilson, 7, tratong, cover

Note to Parents and Teachers

The Let's Take a Field Trip set supports national curriculum standards for social studies related
to institutions, communities, and civic practices. This book describes and illustrates a class field
trip to an airport. The images support early readers in understanding the text. The repetition
of words and phrases helps early readers learn new words. This book also introduces early
readers to subject-specific vocabulary words, which are defined in the Glossary section. Early
readers may need assistance to read some words and to use the Table of Contents, Glossary,
Read More, Internet Sites, Critical Thinking Using the Common Core, and Index sections of
the book.

Printed in the United States of America in Stevens Point, Wisconsin.
092014   008479WZS15

TABLE OF CONTENTS

A SPECIAL SCHOOL DAY

Today is field trip day.

Your class is going to

the airport!

Airports are busy places.
People travel for work
and vacations. Air travel is
the fastest way to go.

INSIDE THE TERMINAL

Travelers stand in line

to check in for their flights.

They check in at computers

or at the ticket counter.

Travelers go through
security inside the terminal.
Security workers search
bags for dangerous items.
This keeps travelers safe.

Passengers wait at the gate.

Finally it is time to board!

Airline employees help

travelers get on the airplane.

C23

UA882 DEPARTS 4:21
BOARDING

C23

UNITED

UNITED

UNITED

13

OUTSIDE THE TERMINAL

Airport workers get

airplanes ready.

They check, fix,

and clean the planes.

Flight control workers

work in towers.

They tell pilots where to go.

TIME FOR TAKEOFF!

Flight attendants work
inside the airplane.
They show passengers how
to be safe on the flight.

Pilots sit in the cockpit.

They work hard to fly

the airplane safely.

A pilot can be a fun

teacher for the day!

GLOSSARY

board—to get inside a vehicle, such as an airplane

cockpit—the place where a pilot sits in a plane

employee—a person who works for a company

field trip—a class visit for learning something new at a place outside school

flight attendant—a person who helps passengers and serves food and drinks on an airplane

flight control worker—a person who helps guide an airplane; flight control workers give pilots directions and other information

pilot—a person who flies a jet or plane

security worker—a person who checks to make sure nothing unsafe gets on airplanes; security workers check travelers' bags and clothing

terminal—a section of an airport

READ MORE

Minden, Cecilia. *Pilots.* Mankato, Minn.: Childs World, 2014.

Parker, Vic. *My First Trip on an Airplane.* Chicago: Heinemann Library, 2011.

Shields, Amy. *Planes.* National Geographic Readers. Washington, D.C.: National Geographic, 2010.

INTERNET SITES

FactHound offers a safe, fun way to find Internet sites related to this book. All of the sites on FactHound have been researched by our staff.

Here's all you do:

Visit *www.facthound.com*

Type in this code: 9781491420959

Super-cool stuff! Check out projects, games and lots more at **www.capstonekids.com**

CRITICAL THINKING
USING THE COMMON CORE

1. What is a flight control worker's job?
(Key Ideas and Details)

2. How is plane travel different from other types of travel?
(Integration of Knowledge and Ideas)

INDEX

Word Count: 150
Grade: 1
Early-Intervention Level: 15